Michael Gow is a writer and director. His writing credits for stage, screen and radio are extensive. His plays include the multi-award-winning *Away*, *The Kid*, *On Top of the World*, *Europe*, *1841*, *Furious*, *Sweet Phoebe*, *Live Acts on Stage*, *The Fortunes of Richard Mahony* and *Toy Symphony*. Between 1999 and 2010 he was Artistic Director of Queensland Theatre Company, where his credits include *Who's Afraid of Virginia Woolf?*, *John Gabriel Borkman*, *Private Fears in Public Places*, *Private Lives* (co-production with State Theatre of South Australia), *Away* (co-production with Griffin Theatre), *Oedipus the King*, *The Venetian Twins*, *The Cherry Orchard*, *The Real Inspector Hound*, *Black Comedy*, *Phedra*, *We Were Dancing*, *The Fortunes of Richard Mahony* (co-production with Playbox), *Cooking with Elvis*, *Bag O' Marbles*, *The Tragedy of King Richard III* (collaboration with The Bell Shakespeare Company), *The Tragedy of King Richard the Second*, *Buried Child*, *Dirt*, *Fred*, *Shopping & F$$$ing*, *Mrs Warren's Profession*, *The Skin of Our Teeth* and *XPO—The Human Factor*, *The Importance of Being Earnest*, *Anatomy Titus Fall of Rome: A Shakespeare Commentary*, *I Am My Own Wife*, *The School of Arts* and *The Crucible*. He has also worked as a director for Sydney Theatre Company, where he was Associate Director from 1991 to 1993, Company B, Black Swan Theatre Company, Griffin Theatre Company, State Theatre Company of South Australia, Australian Theatre for Young People, Playbox, Opera Australia, Sydney Festival and Adelaide Festival.

FURIOUS

Michael Gow

CURRENCY PRESS
The performing arts publisher

CURRENCY PLAYS

First published in Australia in 1994
by Currency Press, PO Box 2287, Strawberry Hills, NSW, 2012, Australia;
enquiries@currency.com.au; www.currency.com.au

This edition first published in 2021.

Cover design by Lisa White.

Currency Press acknowledges the Traditional Owners of the Country on which
we live and work. We pay our respects to all Aboriginal and Torres Strait
Islander Elders, past and present.

A catalogue record for this
book is available from the
National Library of Australia

Furious was originally presented in a staged reading at the Development Site in July 1990 in the Wharf Studio as part of the Development Site program. The director was Dennis Watkins.

Furious was first performed by The Sydney Theatre Company at the Wharf Theatre, Sydney, 6 November 1991 with the following cast:

OLD MAN, FRIEND THREE, BONNY'S HUSBAND, MR MAXWELL, GUS	Peter Corbett
ROLAND	Nicholas Eadie
CONNIE, NURSE, RUTH, LOUISE	Victoria Longley
BRIAN, FRIEND TWO, CHRIS	Tamblyn Lord
LYNNIE, FRIEND ONE	Rachel Szalay
KATHLEEN, ALISON, BONNY, SPOKESPERSON	Kerry Walker

Director, Michael Gow
Assistant Director, Lee Biolos
Designer, Stephen Curtis
Lighting Designer, Mark Howett
Dramaturg, May-Brit Akerholt
Stage Manager, Barbara Durward

CHARACTERS

KATHLEEN	FRIEND THREE
ROLAND	BONNY
NURSE	BONNY'S HUSBAND
YOUNG WOMAN	CHRIS
OLD MAN	SPOKESPERSON
BRIAN	MR MAXWELL
ALISON	LYNNIE
CONNIE	RUTH
FRIEND ONE	LOUISE
FRIEND TWO	GUS

The following doubling is suggested:

ACTOR I: ROLAND

ACTOR II: OLD MAN, FRIEND, BONNIE'S HUSBAND,
    MR MAXWELL, GUS

ACTOR III: BRIAN, FRIEND, CHRIS

ACTOR IV: YOUNG WOMAN, FRIEND, LYNNIE

ACTOR V: KATHLEEN, ALISON, BONNY, SPOKESPERSON

ACTOR VI: CONNIE, NURSE, RUTH, LOUISE

SETTING

In the original production the set consisted of a wall of glass doors
which opened both ways, separating the downstage performing area
from an upstage room, through which all entrances and exits were
made. In the room were one wheelchair and a seventies-style stereo
console from which the tin of photos was produced. Around the walls
of the room at head height was a frieze depicting a desert landscape.
On the downstage acting area was a single armchair, the twin of
the chair in the upstage room. The floor was covered in pale grey
linoleum tiles.

SCENE ONE

Old people's home. ROLAND *enters smoking a cigarette. He looks around the room, then sits. After a moment* KATHLEEN *rushes in.*

KATHLEEN: And where have you been? Where have you been?
ROLAND: I'm sorry, I don't know you.
KATHLEEN: Where have you been?
ROLAND: No. You're mistaking me for someone else, I'm sorry.
KATHLEEN: Out with it! Right here and now.

> *A* NURSE *comes in.*

I want to hear you say it. Now!
NURSE: Stop it. Kathleen, you're a naughty girl. [*To* ROLAND] I'm really sorry, we're so—
KATHLEEN: Where have you been?
NURSE: Stop this now. Stop it. What are you doing here anyway?

> *She goes to the door and calls.*

Brian? Brian! [*To* ROLAND.] We're short staffed. Which one are you here to visit?
ROLAND: No, I'm not visiting anyone, I'm here to collect some things someone—
NURSE: Where is Brian? Never around when you need them. Sorry. You're here to see …
ROLAND: No, I'm not here to see anyone. You contacted me about some things that someone has left for me. Someone who died.
NURSE: Bonny! You're Mr …
ROLAND: Henning.
NURSE: Mr Henning. You're here for Bonny's things. [*To* KATHLEEN] You knew, didn't you? Kathleen was devoted to Bonny. Best friends. Weren't you? Poor old thing. Since Bonny died she's been off the air, permanently furious. Real problem. [*To* KATHLEEN] We get what Bonny left for the man? Back in a sec.

The NURSE *takes* KATHLEEN *off.* ROLAND *is left alone for a moment. A* YOUNG WOMAN *comes in. She is very distressed. She watches* ROLAND *for a moment.*

YOUNG WOMAN: Do you have a cigarette?

ROLAND *gives her a cigarette. He lights it for her. She takes a long drag.*

Thanks.

She goes. ROLAND *paces. An* OLD MAN *shuffles on. He stops in the middle of the room and starts to sway.*

ROLAND: Are you alright?

OLD MAN: Yes.

ROLAND: Should I get someone?

OLD MAN: Yes.

ROLAND *goes to the door and calls.*

ROLAND: Excuse me? Is anyone around? [*Back to the* OLD MAN] Do you want to hold my arm?

OLD MAN: Yes.

ROLAND *offers the* OLD MAN *his arm. Instead, the* OLD MAN *grabs* ROLAND'*s head, staring into his face.* ROLAND *tries to pull away, but the* OLD MAN'*s grip is strong.* BRIAN *comes in.*

BRIAN: What are you doing here? You're in the wrong place. Aren't you?

OLD MAN: Yes.

BRIAN: [*to* ROLAND] All he says. 'Yes. Yes. Yes.' Isn't it?

OLD MAN: Yes.

BRIAN: You're an old cunt, aren't you?

OLD MAN: Yes.

BRIAN: [*laughing*] You can say anything.

BRIAN *and the* OLD MAN *go.* ROLAND *is left alone again for a moment. The* NURSE, *with a clipboard, comes back with* KATHLEEN, *who's carrying a shoe box. She hands the shoe box to* ROLAND.

ROLAND: Thank you.

NURSE: Now back you go, you've given him the box.

> *She goes reluctantly. Just as she is leaving the stage she looks back at* ROLAND.

Can you sign for it please? Here. [*To* KATHLEEN] Off you go now.

ROLAND: Do you know what's in it?

NURSE: Photos mainly. She had them all in the cupboard by her bed. She gathered them all up and put them in the box a couple of days before she died. Old photos are pathetic aren't they? Red Riding Hood. Baptism photo.

ROLAND: Newspaper clippings.

NURSE: Cute baby.

ROLAND: These clippings are all about me.

NURSE: Are you famous?

ROLAND: Not really.

NURSE: Your photo and everything. A writer. What do you write, books?

ROLAND: Plays.

NURSE: TV?

ROLAND: Theatre mainly.

NURSE: Never go. Wow, the papers like you.

ROLAND: This is a photograph of my father. I never knew this woman existed. Why would she leave all this stuff for me? Did you know her well?

NURSE: As well as you could. She never spoke.

ROLAND: Never? How long was she here?

NURSE: Sixteen years. I've only been here three, imagine being stuck here for sixteen. What a way to end your life. I'd rather have a bullet through the brain. Or cyanide. That's the answer.

ROLAND: How did you find me?

NURSE: Some relative of Bonny's. Mrs O'Brien? There's a card I think. Yes. Alison O'Brien. There's a number. Well, back to work. They'll be wandering off into the sunset if I don't get back. This is like a detective show. Good luck.

SCENE TWO

North Shore living room. ALISON *is looking through a small bundle of photographs.*

ALISON: I wouldn't have been more than ten. I remember there were poplar trees. And a low fence. The lawn was always yellow. And the house smelt peculiar. Every time we went there we used to take Auntie Bonny and her little girl to have lunch at the Starlight Milkbar and every time I'd come home disappointed because we didn't see any stars. I had the most fantastical thing dreamed up and it was just an ordinary milkbar. But I remember that feeling of disappointment. Yes, here are the poplars.

ROLAND: Mrs O'Brien, why did Bonny leave these things for me?

ALISON: Both your parents—

ROLAND: My mother five years ago, my father last year.

ALISON: Do you know much about your parents' earlier life?

ROLAND: Not much.

ALISON: I can't imagine my son knowing about me before he entered my life. But you do have a vague sense of what their lives were like?

ROLAND: They were ordinary.

ALISON: Bonny was my aunt, my mother's sister. When she was eighteen she took up with a young man from the country. It was one of those violent youthful passions that always end in chaos. They married and it lasted a year. They had a daughter but the young man left and Bonny raised her daughter alone. Things never improved for poor Bonny. She battled on until her daughter had a child out of wedlock. It was adopted out, the daughter disappeared and Bonny ended up in that home. That was sixteen years ago.

ROLAND: I'm still no clearer why she left all this for me.

ALISON: I asked you about your parents' early life. That's the connection. The young man from the country, Bonny's husband, was your father. Bonny was your father's first wife.

ROLAND: He didn't have a first wife.

ALISON: Yes he did.

ROLAND: Don't be ridiculous, he didn't.

ALISON: I'm sorry, he did.

ROLAND: First. First? My father was married to someone before …

ALISON: Before your mother.

ROLAND: He was married to another—there was another—I never knew.

ALISON: No.

ROLAND: He married someone, left her, never saw her again, left his daughter. I've got a sister.

ALISON: Half sister, yes you have.

ROLAND: What's her name?

ALISON: Lynette. Lynette Henning.

ROLAND: Where is she?

ALISON: No-one knows.

ROLAND: What do you mean no-one knows? Someone must know.

ALISON: No-one.

ROLAND: She was the daughter for fuck's sake.

ALISON: Mr Henning, no-one knows.

ROLAND: Next of kin!

ALISON: There's only me.

ROLAND: Didn't you try to find her?

ALISON: I tried.

ROLAND: What, a couple of phone calls and one visit to the Registry Office?

ALISON: When Bonny went into that home I followed every avenue. Nothing. Lynette just disappeared.

ROLAND: I remember a Sunday afternoon. Winter. I'm still a kid, still at school. The phone rings. My father answers it. His face changes completely. He slams the phone down. Goes to the window. I follow, peer out. There's a woman outside the phone box on the corner of our street staring at our house. He pulls me away from the window, tears me away, nearly throws me across the room. Her. Wanting to see me. As if I were really her child. Have you known about this connection all along?

ALISON: Yes. My mother told me. Bonny knew your father had remarried, settled down. And she knew when you were born, she kept up with you, school, university, career.

ROLAND: She lost her husband, daughter, grandchild, she couldn't speak. No-one. Nothing.

> ROLAND *shivers involuntarily and drops his box of photos, etc.*

ALISON: You need to take all of this in very slowly. Come back whenever you want. Actually … you could help me as well. Chris, my son, is in his last year at school. Chris isn't much of a scholar, he works hard though, but … he's not … fantastic. He has to study one of your plays at school … perhaps you could help him. It wouldn't take long. Just a few questions. Whenever it suited you, whenever you feel you're ready to find out more about Bonny. What do you think? Mr Henning?

ROLAND: [*shivering*] Where's that draught coming from?

ALISON: So what do you think about helping with my son's education?

ROLAND: Yes of course, that will be … yes.

ALISON: [*as she hands his box back*] Wonderful.

SCENE THREE

Fashionable apartment.

CONNIE: I didn't know if you were sick—

ROLAND: I wasn't sick, no—

CONNIE: I didn't know how much you'd had to drink. The waiter seemed to be in a holding pattern over our table. Another out-of-work actor on the make.

ROLAND: Who?

CONNIE: That waiter.

ROLAND: What waiter?

CONNIE: Earring. Ponytail.

ROLAND: Connie, what are you talking about?

CONNIE: Where the fuck have you been? I am absolutely furious.

You disappeared straight after you got the award. Won't do your career any good, you didn't even wait to see who got Poetry. Sitting there, feeling like a complete total fucking idiot. You just left me there, this empty chair gaping next to me for an hour and a half.

ROLAND: I must be coming down with something, I've caught something, a chill, do people still catch chills? I'm cold all the time, and there's this rushing sound in my ears, not like blood pumping, it's not my pulse, just this ... rushing. Tonight I was looking around the room at all those arts administrators and politicians listening to the Premier droning on about how important the arts are to a healthy community and suddenly I started shivering and first I thought 'the oysters' and my heart sank because I thought I was in for a night in the toilet and then I realised he was saying my name, twice ... three times—

CONNIE: This is why I thought you were—

ROLAND: So I got up and stumbled towards the Premier—

CONNIE: Exactly, this is why I thought you were—

ROLAND: Up the stairs and as he offered his hand to shake there was this terrific blast of cold air, freezing, ice, and this noise like a hurricane coming. I couldn't hear what he said to me. Then I tried to offer him my hand and I froze, I couldn't give him my hand ... and the air was so ... so—

CONNIE: Yes I saw you hesitate—

ROLAND: [*gives up*] Cold. I had to get out of there, get warm.

CONNIE: It was the air conditioning turning over.

ROLAND: Yes of course, thank you Connie. That explains everything.

He clears his throat.

Is anyone else still here?

CONNIE: No-one important, just us, just your closest friends.

ROLAND: Connie, would you have ever thought of my father as a man with a secret past?

CONNIE: No, but I never thought my father was the type to dress up in women's clothes and wear make up, but he did. In the war.

ROLAND: Last week I was contacted by this old people's home, terrible place. This woman I'd never heard of died and left a box for me. In the box were photos from this woman's life and all these newspaper clippings about me, from way back.

He clears his throat, then falls silent a moment.

CONNIE: How did they find you?

ROLAND: A relative. This woman … niece? Yes, the dead woman's niece. I went to see her. She unreeled this family saga. The punchline was, this dead woman was Dad's first wife.

CONNIE: Did you know he had one?

ROLAND: Of course I didn't know, what a stupid question. I dug out his marriage certificate. Here.

He takes the certificate from a pocket and hands it to her.

No mention, just my mother. But look closer, hold it up to the light.

She does.

CONNIE: There's a mark.

ROLAND: He scratched out the name of his first wife with a blade, carefully, meticulously scratched her out of his life. My father left her with a daughter, my half sister. Her name's Lynette. Lynette Henning. Dad's first wife, Bonny, brought my sister up alone. Then my sister got pregnant, adopted the kid out and just disappeared. Bonny ended up in this terrible home, isn't that a great word for places like that, home? Such a hopeless, pointless, meaningless life.

CONNIE: This is a shock.

ROLAND groans impatiently.

I mean … shock. You are in shock. You need time to think. It's huge, monumental.

ROLAND: I'm cold.

CONNIE: Go in to the fire.

ROLAND: No, I don't want to see anyone.

He clears his throat.

CONNIE: You should be happy tonight, happy and drunk. Roland, most of those people at that thing hadn't read the winning novel, hadn't even heard of the winning poet, but they'd seen your plays. And every single one of those people who said how much they loved your work actually meant it. You give people something Roland.

ROLAND: I'm starting to write something.

CONNIE: No you're not, you're never like this when you first start work on something. You grow taller, you glow when something starts to form.

ROLAND: I've been carrying that marriage certificate around for three days. It's worn a hole right through me, like a blade in my pocket, cutting into me. That woman gave something to me, so that I can give something back to her, so I can give her life meaning. I mustn't ignore it.

CONNIE: God if you think you have to turn every little thing that happens to you into a play you'll go crazy.

ROLAND: This is not a little thing!

CONNIE: I didn't mean this in particular.

ROLAND: You open your mouth and such crap comes out.

CONNIE: What could you make out of this woman's life? It sounds completely depressing, total failure. Not what you write about. Imagine sitting through something like that. Leave it in the real world and get over it.

ROLAND: Don't you say that to me. How dare you.

CONNIE: Roland—

ROLAND: Don't you ever, ever order me around again.

He clears his throat.

Basking in reflected glory, living by proxy. I hate the way you cling to me to give your own life meaning. You know what my agent calls you? The Minion. 'How's The Minion?' he always asks, 'I suppose The Minion will be there tonight', 'Did The Minion enjoy the show? But of course The Minion always does, that's what minions are for.' Everything I do is just something to fill your own void. You suck my blood. Fuck I'm cold.

He clears his throat.

Can you hear that?

CONNIE: What?

ROLAND: That wind?

FRIEND ONE *enters with a medal.*

FRIEND ONE: Congratulations! Give me a kiss, clever boy, clever, clever boy.

FRIEND TWO *enters.*

FRIEND TWO: Where've you been hiding?

FRIEND ONE: Another ugly piece of metal. Who designs these things? Hiiiiideous!

FRIEND THREE *enters.*

FRIEND THREE: We're all pissed as farts by now!

ROLAND *clears his throat.*

FRIEND TWO: What's up?

FRIEND ONE: Caught cold, clever boy. That will teach you to walk out of state ceremonies without your muff.

ROLAND *clears his throat again.*

FRIEND TWO: Roland are you all right?

FRIEND THREE: Bit of tax payer's food stuck in your craw?

FRIEND TWO: Try the Heimlich Manoeuvre.

FRIEND ONE & FRIEND THREE: [*together*] The what?

FRIEND TWO: When someone's choking. You stand behind them, wrap your arms around their diaphragms and pull.

ROLAND: I'm alright.

FRIEND THREE: Do you do that in public or wait till you've got them home?

FRIEND ONE: Roland doesn't wear a diaphragm, do you Roland?

ROLAND *clears his throat.*

FRIEND TWO: You sure you're alright?

CONNIE: He's started a new play.

FRIEND THREE: God! The old creative juices at work again?

FRIEND ONE: [*simultaneously*] And you've only just got the award for the last one.

FRIEND ONE: Any hints?

CONNIE: Something completely different it seems.
ROLAND: [*to* CONNIE] Go to hell.
CONNIE: Fuck you.
FRIEND TWO: Is everything alright?
ROLAND: [*shouts*]And where have you been?

> *Silence.*

FRIEND ONE: Is Roland turning into Linda Blair?
ROLAND: Let me out.

> *He goes.*

CONNIE: Good night.

SCENE FOUR

Bonny's house. Her HUSBAND *has a suitcase.*

BONNY: Where have you been?
HUSBAND: Don't worry about it, Bonny.
BONNY: You're so late.
HUSBAND: Sorry.
BONNY: Come inside.
HUSBAND: No.
BONNY: Why not?
HUSBAND: Just came for a last look.
BONNY: Tell me where you've been.
HUSBAND: The railway.
BONNY: What for?
HUSBAND: To buy a ticket.
BONNY: For the train?
HUSBAND: A train ticket, yes.
BONNY: Where to?
HUSBAND: You think I'd tell you.
BONNY: Where to?
HUSBAND: Away from here. Away from you.
BONNY: You going back to the bush?
HUSBAND: No comment as they say in the papers.

BONNY: Where?

HUSBAND: I told you—

BONNY: Tell me!

HUSBAND: I'm not telling you a thing.

BONNY: What about Lynnie?

HUSBAND: All yours.

BONNY: She's ours.

HUSBAND: Not any more.

BONNY: You can't leave us.

HUSBAND: Yes I can. Yes I can. And for once just shut up and listen. I'm going. I don't know where. Just so long as it's away from you. I don't want to spend another minute near you. You drive me crazy, you drive me round the bend. Everything's a battle with you, the smallest thing is like the war all over again and I don't want any more. I don't care what happens as long as I don't have to fight out another thing with you. I'm going where I can have some peace and quiet. Find someone to live with who keeps their mouth shut. I want to say what I want and no arguments. You want someone to argue with, over every single thing that happens, fight with the kid, do it to her. And don't try begging, saying sorry. Just more talk. I've had that up to here, Bonny, enough of that to last a lifetime.

BONNY: And what do I do?

HUSBAND: You're on your own.

SCENE FIVE

North Shore living room. ROLAND *is wearing a jumper and is looking at a small bundle of photographs.* CHRIS *has books and a notebook.*

CHRIS: Umm. Mr Henning.

ROLAND: Roland.

CHRIS: I'm sorry about this. I didn't know Mum was going to line this up.

ROLAND: Don't worry.

CHRIS: I'll just ask you these questions. Umm. In your play … we have to study your play at school.

ROLAND: I'm sorry.

CHRIS: [*laughing*] In your play, does the character of the young man represent loss of innocence?

ROLAND: No.

Pause. CHRIS*'s smile fades.*

CHRIS: What does the character of the young man represent?

ROLAND: Nothing. Except maybe a young man.

CHRIS: Does the play have universality in its depiction of family tension?

ROLAND: No.

CHRIS: Does the ending suggest the restoration of cosmic order?

ROLAND: No. Are these your questions?

CHRIS: They're some of the things our teacher says. I just turned them into questions. Umm. Did you or anyone you know go through the same things the family goes through in the play?

ROLAND: Yes.

CHRIS: Great.

ROLAND: And no.

CHRIS: Oh.

ROLAND: How old are you?

CHRIS: Sixteen.

ROLAND: You're less than half my age.

CHRIS: Yeah?

ROLAND: Yeah.

Pause.

CHRIS: Dad wants me to do better at school, get better marks, get ahead. Mum'll do anything to help me achieve.

ROLAND: Achieve what?

CHRIS: Something.

ROLAND: What are you going to do when you leave school?

CHRIS: I dunno. Do you hate knowing all these kids are asking these questions about what you wrote?

ROLAND: I hate knowing you're all being fed crap by school teachers.

CHRIS: Another question?

ROLAND: Yes.

CHRIS: What does the lost brother in the play stand for?

ROLAND: Stand for?

CHRIS: That's the way the teachers talk.

ROLAND: Nothing stands for anything. Everything is.

CHRIS: Is the basic theme of your play individual personal growth towards acceptance—

ROLAND: Jesus.

CHRIS: What?

ROLAND: You want to know the basic theme of the play? You want to know the basic theme of everything that's ever been written?

> ROLAND *goes straight to him, lifts him up and kisses him.* CHRIS *doesn't move.* ROLAND *releases* CHRIS *but, after the briefest moment,* CHRIS *pulls* ROLAND *back and kisses him.*

You're so warm. Where's your room?

CHRIS: [*leading* ROLAND *towards his room*] Oh shit, man. I'm in the rowing team.

SCENE SIX

Bonny's house. She has a pram.

BONNY: The house is quiet. I've never heard the house this quiet. But it's our house, Lynnie. We'll stay here. It's not good for a child to move around. You need to know where your home is. I'll make sure we stay. Whatever it takes. I'll work. We can manage. We won't need much. Two of us. I know I can do it. I have to. This is what my life will be. You're mine and I'm all you have. That's all there is. We don't need anyone else. We don't need anyone.

> *She wheels the pram offstage.*

SCENE SEVEN

Conference room. ROLAND *in thick jacket and scarf, is reading to a group of people.*

ROLAND: 'The house is quiet. I've never heard the house this quiet. But it's our house Lynnie. We'll stay here. It's not good for a child to move around. You need to know where your home is. I'll make sure we stay. Whatever it takes. I'll work. We can manage. We won't need much. Two of us. I know I can do it. I have to. This is what my life will be. You're mine and I'm all you have. That's all there is. We don't need anyone else. We don't need anyone. She wheels the pram offstage.' Thank you.

SPOKESPERSON: No, thank you Mr Henning. Ah, I know I speak for everyone when I say how exciting it was to hear from a new play of yours, as always. Ah, your readings have been a high point of this theatre conference for nearly a decade, since your first one. We certainly are looking forward to seeing this one up and running. [*To the others*] Ah, now that's the last in the Works in Progress series, last but by no means least. So if you'd join with me in thanking Mr Roland Henning for reading for us today. [*Applause*] Ah, now, before we break for lunch, there are a couple of messages from the Conference office. Ah, this afternoon's forum Towards a Non-Threatening Theatre has been moved to the canteen and the Puppetry workshop has unfortunately been cancelled, which is a great shame. Ah, and anyone who would like to register for the Grotesque Acting classes and who hasn't done so can do so at the office until four. Thank you. Thank you Roland.

They all go except for MR MAXWELL.

MR MAXWELL: That was interesting. You usually end up with us all in fits of laughter.

ROLAND: Mr Maxwell. Where's Mrs Maxwell?

MR MAXWELL: She couldn't come.

ROLAND: Oh?

MR MAXWELL: She's gone back into hospital.

ROLAND: I'm very sorry.

MR MAXWELL: One of the nurses took me aside and said she didn't think I should go too far away, but Eleanor insisted I come. She was so disappointed she couldn't be here. You remember last time we talked? The Festival?

ROLAND: Yes.

MR MAXWELL: Someone in the audience asked you if you had a personal theory of drama and you said, 'Drama is a Greek word meaning hurry up get on with it.' She loved that.

ROLAND: Yes I remember.

MR MAXWELL: So even though she was too sick to be here she didn't want us both to miss out.

ROLAND: I see.

MR MAXWELL: Shall we work here?

ROLAND: Mr Maxwell. I'm afraid I can't talk to you about your play.

MR MAXWELL: Didn't you get it?

ROLAND: I got it.

MR MAXWELL: I posted it over a month ago.

ROLAND: I got it.

MR MAXWELL: She typed it herself, ill as she was, stayed up two nights.

ROLAND: I got it.

MR MAXWELL: Haven't you read it?

ROLAND: Yes, I read it and started—

MR MAXWELL: Didn't you like it?

ROLAND: It doesn't have anything to do with how I—

MR MAXWELL: Is it the ending? I thought having our son coming to the hospital, straight from the airport, all the way from America still carrying his luggage … I thought it was very moving.

ROLAND: It would be.

MR MAXWELL: You think it's no good.

ROLAND: Mr Maxwell, in the end, how I feel about it as a piece of writing is irrelevant.

MR MAXWELL: It means everything. It's been you that's kept me writing. Encouragement, feedback, always pushing me to do better.

ROLAND: Yes, I know that. But now I'm working myself—

MR MAXWELL: You're tired, aren't you?

ROLAND: Not tired.

MR MAXWELL: It's lunch now and there's not that much on this afternoon. Why don't we find somewhere quiet, have a bite to eat and read through it later?

ROLAND: No.

MR MAXWELL: Or would you like a coffee?

ROLAND: Mr Maxwell—

MR MAXWELL: A drink?

ROLAND: Mr Maxwell. You must stop writing this play.

MR MAXWELL: What?

ROLAND: I like you very much, I like both of you. It always gave me pleasure to see your faces somewhere in the audience, I loved getting your letters, I even enjoyed helping you write your play. And that's why I want you to stop. Because I don't want you to be hurt.

MR MAXWELL: I can take criticism, you know that.

ROLAND: This isn't criticism. This is the truth. Please listen to me Mr Maxwell, something's happening to me, I can't help you any more, I can't see you any more, it's too dangerous for you, trust me, just go back to Mrs Maxwell, care for her, be with her—

MR MAXWELL: She wants to know what you think. I can't go back to the hospital and tell her you said stop writing it. You know how important this play is to her. I'm convinced it's what kept her going this long. And knowing you like what I'm writing means an enormous amount, I can't tell you. Don't send me away empty handed.

ROLAND: Please try and understand I can't help you now.

MR MAXWELL: Let's read the last scene at least.

ROLAND: You have no idea what you're really dealing with.

MR MAXWELL: You have an obligation to read my play.

ROLAND: I had an obligation to read at this idiotic conference. I've done that. I had an obligation to talk to you. I have done that. I have no more obligations. Now I'm leaving.

MR MAXWELL: You can't walk away like that.

ROLAND: I have to! I beg you, let me go.

MR MAXWELL: You have to give me something to tell my wife.

ROLAND: Tell her the truth Mr Maxwell! Tell her you can't write. Tell her I was a coward, I should never have encouraged you in the first place. The moment you started to waste an entire forest getting this garbage off your chest I should have said, 'Stop. Go no further'. But I was a coward. I'm very sorry. You want something to tell your wife? Tell her you couldn't write a shopping list. Tell her you couldn't write 'fuck' on a dirty Venetian blind. Tell her your son will never come home from America, she will never see him again, she'll die without ever seeing him again.

MR MAXWELL: How can you say that?

ROLAND: I don't know. I just open my mouth and out it comes. I'm sorry. Mr Maxwell, I tried to warn you.

MR MAXWELL: May I have my manuscript back?

ROLAND: Of course. I'm sorry. Please try and understand—

MR MAXWELL: I understand perfectly. Thank you for your time. Goodbye.

SCENE EIGHT

Bonny's house.

BONNY: And where have you been?

LYNNIE: What are you doing home?

BONNY: Where have you been?

LYNNIE: It's Wednesday.

BONNY: I know what day it is.

LYNNIE: Why aren't you at the club?

BONNY: I knocked off early. Where have you been?

LYNNIE: Out.

BONNY: I saw you Lynnie. Coming out of the Starlight Milkbar.

LYNNIE: I went in to have a cup of tea.

BONNY: Who with?

LYNNIE: No-one.

BONNY: Who was the man that came out with you?

LYNNIE: I don't know.

BONNY: You were yelling at him. Come here.

LYNNIE: Mum …

BONNY: Come here I said!

> LYNNIE *goes to* BONNY.

You've been crying.

LYNNIE: No I haven't, I'm a bit tired.

BONNY: I saw you in the street hanging onto a man and bawling your eyes out! Who was he?

> LYNNIE *shrugs.*

BONNY: I went to the doctor too. My tablets nearly ran out. He said congratulations, how excited I must be now I'm going to be a grandma.

LYNNIE: He wasn't supposed to tell you! I always knew that old doctor was an idiot. It was going to be a surprise. That's … That's what Gus and me were arguing about: when to tell everyone … about us getting married and the baby. I'm sorry. We had to get married in secret. His family. They're very high up, really rich, and they wanted Gus to marry someone high up like them, so we did it in secret. They don't know yet either.

BONNY: Show me the marriage certificate.

LYNNIE: Now?

BONNY: If you're married, you must have a marriage certificate.

LYNNIE: I've got one.

BONNY: Show me.

LYNNIE: I can't remember where I put it.

BONNY: Married!

LYNNIE: I am. I am. I am! I'll show you. Where did I put it?

> *She goes out.*

We went to the marriage place, Gus didn't want to have it in a church. There was just us and the man that does the marriages.

She comes back in with a biscuit tin.

Now, I put it in here, I'm sure. Here's all my baby photos. Here's my baptism photo. We are married.

She scatters things all over the floor as she searches.

Here's me in the infants' school. Here's me as Red Riding Hood. Here's all my school reports. Here's photos of Dad. Of course! Gus's got it.

She stuffs all the photos and papers back into the tin.

God I'm stupid. Fancy forgetting that. Yeah … Gus hung onto it. That's where it is. What a dumbo. I got so worried. I'll put this away. Wait till you see our wedding picture.

She takes the tin off.

Then you'll believe me, won't you?

BONNY: Yes.

SCENE NINE

Roland's place. There's loud pop music from sixteen years ago.
ROLAND *wears a heavy jumper and fingerless gloves.*

ROLAND: That's too loud! I told you the rules if you want to come here in the afternoons.

CHRIS: Where does this music come from? Couldn't believe it, stuck away in the middle of all the Mahler and Shostakovich. Do you like this stuff?

ROLAND: It was too loud.

CHRIS: But you actually like it?

ROLAND: I've been listening to the music that was around sixteen years ago. I'm trying to work.

CHRIS: How's it going?

ROLAND: How do you think, this stuff blasting my ears off?

CHRIS: You've got the shits.

ROLAND: I'm trying to work.

CHRIS: It was so quiet. Just the clock ticking. What am I supposed to do?

ROLAND: What you came here to do.

CHRIS: We did that.

ROLAND: I told you you could come here as long as you were quiet when I'm working.

CHRIS: You're not working now. We could do it again.

ROLAND: I can't.

CHRIS: Worn out?

ROLAND: Go home.

CHRIS: Now?

ROLAND: Now. We have to stop this.

CHRIS: You started it.

ROLAND: Then I'm stopping it.

CHRIS: Is that how you treat everyone? Chuck them away when you've had enough? Walk away? Thanks for nothing?

ROLAND: This is too risky.

CHRIS: We're careful, we do all the right things.

ROLAND: Morally risky.

CHRIS: Are you kidding?

ROLAND: This is probably child abuse. In fifteen years you'll start cutting old ladies' fingers off and they'll trace it all back to me.

CHRIS: You're crazy.

ROLAND: And this old writer, young boy—

CHRIS: You're not old—

ROLAND: —teacher pupil thing, art history, poetry, music appreciation … before long we'll be shopping for antiques together and subscribing to the opera. I'll end up dying in a deck chair on the beach with my make-up running down my face. It's not me. So let's stop before we really damage each other.

CHRIS: I'm just getting the blame because your writing's not going very well is it?

ROLAND: No.

CHRIS: Why?

ROLAND: Why? Because writers work in solitude, in silence and I've got this sixteen year old athlete raging around my lounge room. Driving me crazy. You shouldn't be here.

CHRIS: But I am and you love it, don't you? Say yes, Roland.

CHRIS *twists* ROLAND*'s nipple.*

ROLAND: [*finally giving in*] Yes, Roland.

CHRIS: Now. The truth. What's wrong with your writing?

ROLAND: The further I go, the darker it gets. The path keeps going down. You better go.

CHRIS: Roland, have you ever felt like you were two people? More than two, ten, fifty? I never felt like one person until I met you. It's always been in my head, the stuff we do and not just that, all kinds of stuff I've imagined doing. It's like what I want to do has always been just over there, all I'd have to do'd be reach for it, but I have to stop myself, too scared. So there's the me at home, studying, eating dinner with Mum and Dad, sailing on the weekend, rowing practice, church. And then there's the me at the beach looking at bodies all the time, me in the showers at school, me every night alone in bed. But here I know where I am. It's like I'm all here all at once, at the same time. So if I shut up, complete silence, I can stay, I can keep coming back? Have you got a spare key? I can come and go and if you're working you won't even have to stop and let me in. You can stay in your room. You won't know I'm here, until you need a break, a breather. Otherwise, silence, study. Here, see, this is me studying.

SCENE TEN

Bonny's house. The same music as in Scene Nine is playing loudly.
BONNY *comes in.*

BONNY: Oh, terrible noise! [*Turning the music off*] What a racket. There little man, all noisy and awful. Lynnie! Lynnie this second.

She goes back to the pram, looks in.

You'll go deaf as a post, awful music.

LYNNIE *comes in.*

You left the radio on in here, full blast, he'll go deaf.

LYNNIE: Sounded just right from where I was.

BONNY: You're lucky you've got me to look after this baby.

LYNNIE: You won't have to worry much longer. What's the time?

BONNY: After four.

LYNNIE: They're late.

BONNY: What have you done?

LYNNIE: Thought they'd've come and gone while you were still out. Typical, government people.

BONNY: Lynnie you didn't.

LYNNIE: Gus has got a job out west, some town, he's going, he wants me and he wants me on my own. Got that? I'm going. Best thing, give the kid a new start, better than I can, we'll get over it.

BONNY: You're just saying this to upset me. Don't even say it mucking around.

LYNNIE: Not mucking around.

She goes out.

I started this mess on a Wednesday so I thought I may as well finish it on a Wednesday as well. I saw the welfare people, talked to them for hours, signed the papers.

She comes back with a bag.

Bag's packed, got what I need, took some things—starting a home, need a few things, you won't use them.

BONNY: He's mine. I've done everything. Since the first day.

LYNNIE: He's not yours, mum, he's mine, an' he's going.

BONNY: No. I'll look after … I will, don't do this, go after Gus, go wherever you want, please Lynnie, please, oh please. I swear I'd look after him, he would be that happy with me, we'd be fine, the two of us, don't let them take him, don't don't.

A knock at the door.

LYNNIE: About time.

BONNY: Shhhhh. We'll pretend we're not here. Get down. They'll go away.

LYNNIE: No it's for the best.

BONNY: Just wait a little while, at least, we'll work something out.

LYNNIE *opens the door.* RUTH *enters.*

LYNNIE: Hello Ruth. He's there, all clean, ready to go.

RUTH: [*aware of the tension in the room*] It's very wise, what your daughter's doing, it's the best step.

LYNNIE: We both know that now.

RUTH: You won't see him again. You understand that, don't you?

LYNNIE: Oh yes.

RUTH: [*to* BONNY] It is for the best, isn't it?

RUTH *goes out with the baby.*

LYNNIE: Gone. Maybe we should've sent all the nappies and stuff. No, they probably don't pass stuff on like that to the new owners. So. I'm going. To Gus. Right?

BONNY: Yes.

LYNNIE: You can look after yourself. You'll manage, won't you.

She goes out.

BONNY: Yes.

SCENE ELEVEN

Room in university building. ROLAND *is in a jacket, scarf, gloves and beanie.*

LOUISE: I'm sorry I'm late. I had a class, they wanted to talk.

ROLAND: It's fine, I went to the library.

LOUISE: Discussing the French influences on a dead writer while you're keeping a live one waiting.

ROLAND: You're here now. Where are they?

LOUISE: They're still in the box you brought them in. For some reason I've decided the box is as important as the manuscripts. The contrast, I suppose, all the drafts of your plays in an old cardboard carton. I don't think I've told you yet how grateful I am. For being able to look through all these drafts of your work. You've been very generous. It's at the printers now, actually, as we speak. I had a terrible time thinking of a title for it. I really didn't want to give it the usual weighty title that screams 'boring doctoral thesis'. Because ... well ... it's not a boring doctoral thesis it's ... a rivetting doctoral thesis.

ROLAND: There's a clue in here somewhere.

LOUISE: To what?

ROLAND: How it's done.

LOUISE: How what's done?

ROLAND: Just tell me where it is.

LOUISE: Where what is?

ROLAND: The clue.

LOUISE: You'll have to give me a little more, Roland, which clue to what?

ROLAND: Tell me what I do.

LOUISE: What you do?

ROLAND: Yes.

LOUISE: You mean write?

ROLAND: Yes, how?

LOUISE: I think you use a word processor now don't you, I guess you tap your fingers on the keys.

ROLAND: Tell me! I need to know. What do I do? Describe it.

LOUISE: You take familiar lives, in a family context and ... illuminate them? Transfigure them? ... um, by ... creating a comic surface—this is all just coming straight out of my thesis.

ROLAND: Go on!

LOUISE: Well ... I suppose you create this comic surface, and through comedy and without totally resolving anything thematically ... um, this comic mode, the comic framework, allows for a sense of renewal—

ROLAND: Renewal. Restore. Replenish. Regenerate. Redeem. While I was in the library I hauled all the dictionaries off the shelves and sat on the floor and looked all these words up. 'To make new again. To restore to a former state. To fill up again. To give back or return. To heal. Release, ransom. To recreate. To give fresh life.'

He drops to the floor and begins tearing through the manuscripts.

I looked up old newspapers and reread reviews. 'Henning Lifts

Our Hearts Again.' 'A Joyous Night of Theatre Magic.' I sat
and read exam papers. 'Henning's vision is essentially sunny,
though the shadows are sometimes long.' Expand and discuss.
But no clue. Nothing.

LOUISE: What's happened?

ROLAND: I'm writing a play.

LOUISE: What?

ROLAND: I'm writing a play.

LOUISE: Now?

ROLAND: Yes.

LOUISE: You didn't tell me.

ROLAND: I'm sorry.

LOUISE: A new play.

ROLAND: Yes.

LOUISE: A new play. Is it finished?

ROLAND: Not yet.

LOUISE: Can I see it?

ROLAND: No.

LOUISE: Just look at it?

ROLAND: I told you.

LOUISE: I know, but if I could at least get a feel—

ROLAND: I said no!

LOUISE: I'm sorry. What's it about?

ROLAND: My family.

LOUISE: That's good. Good.

ROLAND: You think so?

LOUISE: You're staying with that theme, that's good.

ROLAND: You approve do you?

LOUISE: Why didn't you mention this, at least warn me?

ROLAND: I didn't know. Suddenly I was in the middle of it.

LOUISE: Tell me how like your others it is. Does it feel like new
ground?

ROLAND: Yes!

LOUISE: Are you saying my basic argument is already out of date?

ROLAND: I don't know, am I?

LOUISE: Why didn't you tell me?

ROLAND: Because this is bigger than a fucking Ph.D.

LOUISE: All this time and energy describing your 'comic vision' and you come in here and tell me you've reached a major turning point in your work! A crisis! The most exciting thing that could possibly happen. And someone else will get to describe it! This is fucking wonderful. Think Louise, think, think. [*Pacing*] What am I going to do? What am I supposed to do now? What, Roland?

ROLAND: Stop asking me. I want *you* to tell *me* something.

LOUISE: I can't believe this.

ROLAND: Tell me how I do what I do.

LOUISE: I'd have to say I'm feeling a bit betrayed.

ROLAND: I can't bear writing this play.

LOUISE: A bit? A lot betrayed.

ROLAND: I'm afraid. Help me.

LOUISE: Me? Help you? You gave me all your manuscripts to help me write my thesis. But that's not a box of plays, it's a bomb. And it just exploded. All the work I've done!

ROLAND: You know more about me than I do. Help me.

LOUISE: What with, writer's block?

ROLAND: I wish it was a block. But I can't stop what's spewing out. I'm lost in it, it's dragging me along, pulling me under. I'm cold. I'm afraid.

LOUISE: You want to find a clue, take them away and look for it. I won't be needing them. They're yours, take them. Go on, get them out of my sight! I'm sorry, I can't help you. If there is a clue, I don't know where it is. You want a clue? Find it yourself.

She goes.

SCENE TWELVE

Bonny's house.

RUTH: Do you know your name?
BONNY: Yes.
RUTH: What is it?

BONNY: Yes.

RUTH: No. Tell me your name. What is your name?

BONNY: Yes.

RUTH: How long have you been on your own?

BONNY: Yes.

RUTH: I'm going to take you somewhere, Bonny. Do you understand?

BONNY: Yes.

RUTH: You can't stay here on your own like this. I'll take you somewhere where you'll be comfortable. And you'll have something to eat. Then we'll find your family.

    BONNY *reacts.*

You understand?

BONNY: Yes.

SCENE THIRTEEN

Roland's place. ROLAND *wrapped in a doona, listening to loud classical music.* ALISON *enters and turns off the music.*

ALISON: Mothers would make the best detectives. They'd soon solve most cases. Clues, Mr Henning. The tiniest things give people away and mothers notice more than anyone. Anticipation is a pretty clear sign. That's because we've all wanted time to pass quicker so that we can rush off to be with someone. Then there's the name repeated once too often in the one sentence. A subject brought into the discussion simply so that that name can be repeated. Yes, that's a real giveaway, the name. Music. Played too loud, or taken off as soon as someone else comes into the house, music that's never been listened to before. And why would my son wear a key pinned inside his school blazer?

    She throws the key on the floor.

There are no secrets from mothers.

ROLAND: What did you expect to find? Something bloodstained?

Some metal object caked in something? There's just me. Where's Chris?

ALISON: I thought your job was to create. You've done nothing but destroy.

ROLAND: I gave your son an education.

ALISON: You destroyed my family. I'm going to tell everyone about you. I want every gutter newspaper to know, every journalist on television, every sensational news program to expose you.

ROLAND: You won't tell anyone about me. Because you don't really care what I do with your son. You don't care that I love to bury my face in his arse because he's so hot. You don't really care that when I've got his cock in my fist and the cum's running down my fingers, he leans his head back and laughs and says, 'Oh shit, man.' You don't even care that he gives a little grunt when I first shove it in.

ALISON: Stop it.

ROLAND: I got closer to him than you. I've seen him do things you'll never see. I've seen him happier than you ever will.

ALISON *slaps* ROLAND.

I love your son.

ALISON: If I had a gun, I'd kill you.

ROLAND *rushes out.*

SCENE FOURTEEN

Old people's home. RUTH *leads* BONNY *into the room. She takes off* BONNY*'s coat.*

RUTH: This is a nice coat.

RUTH *indicates* BONNY *should sit.* BONNY *does.*

You'll settle in here, won't you?

BONNY: Yes.

RUTH *goes. The light goes out.* BONNY *sits alone in the silence. After a while,* ROLAND *comes in.*

ROLAND: Are you awake? Shhh. It's alright … No, no, don't be afraid. Shhh. It's me. You know me, don't you?

BONNY: Yes.

ROLAND: Yes. We're going for a drive. Into the night. I'll put your life back together. I've got a map, see. I know where she lives. [*Spreading a map out on the floor*] She lives … somewhere … a tiny spot … there! I hope you like fast cars; that's what we're going in. You might need a scarf, the wind'll blow your hair around. What do you want to put on? This coat?

BONNY: Yes.

ROLAND: Put it on then. Here. Up you hop and put it on. Come on. Time. Hurry. Everything?

BONNY: Yes!

ROLAND: Shhh. We'd better be quiet. Something monumental is happening.

> *They go. The music heard at the beginning of Scene Thirteen is heard again.*

SCENE FIFTEEN

Gus and Lynnie's place.

GUS: Come away from the window.

LYNNIE: I bathe your hands.

GUS: Always staring out. What's there to see?

LYNNIE: Gus.

GUS: What are you waiting to see?

LYNNIE: Nothing. Are they sore?

GUS: Yes.

LYNNIE: Worse?

GUS: They can't get worse. They won't get better and they can't get worse.

LYNNIE: I'll bathe them.

> *She begins to take the bandages off his hands.*

GUS: I know why you're always at the window.

LYNNIE: Yeah?

GUS: I know what you think about.

LYNNIE: You do not.

GUS: Yes I do. We read each other's minds. We know everything that passes through our heads.

LYNNIE: I stopped reading yours a long time ago.

GUS: Did you now?

LYNNIE: Got bored. Same thing over and over. Boring.

GUS: I still read yours.

LYNNIE: I know you do. I can feel it.

GUS: And you know what I hear?

LYNNIE: What?

GUS: Sixteen years. The kid. That's all you think about.

LYNNIE: Really?

GUS: The kid. Yep, that's it.

LYNNIE: Shutup.

GUS: I'm right, aren't I?

LYNNIE: Maybe.

GUS: I was, I was right.

LYNNIE: Hold still.

GUS: The only thing you think about.

LYNNIE: What else is there? Stuck here?

GUS: You're not stuck.

LYNNIE: That's right.

GUS: You can go.

LYNNIE: Yes.

GUS: Any time.

LYNNIE: Any time I like.

GUS: Just go.

LYNNIE: Just up and go. Whenever.

GUS: Whenever you like.

They both start to laugh.

LYNNIE: Out that door, that's right.

GUS: That's right.

LYNNIE: Someone's coming. There's a car.

GUS: No-one's coming.

LYNNIE: No, there's a car. Someone's coming.

GUS: We'll pretend we're not here. Come away.

LYNNIE: No. Someone's coming! At last! Someone's coming! I knew someone would finally come.

GUS: Get down, they'll go away.

LYNNIE: Two of them. No, oh no.

GUS: Who is it?

Enter ROLAND *and* BONNY.

ROLAND: Are you Lynette Henning?

LYNNIE: Yes.

ROLAND: Do you know who this is?

LYNNIE: Yes I do.

GUS: I'll say she does.

LYNNIE: Shut up.

ROLAND: Bonny? You know who this is?

BONNY: Yes.

ROLAND: It's Lynnie.

GUS: What are you, some kind of social worker or something?

ROLAND: And you're Gus, aren't you?

GUS: Give the man a medal.

LYNNIE: Shutup I said.

ROLAND: Here she is, Lynette.

LYNNIE: Look—

ROLAND: Say hello, Bonny. Can you say that?

BONNY: Yes.

GUS: Oh, this is really touching.

LYNNIE: Gus.

ROLAND: She's very tired.

LYNNIE: Gus get out of the chair.

GUS: So sorry. Here.

ROLAND *seats* BONNY.

ROLAND: They went to check up on you and found her alone in the house. She's been in a … in a home for sixteen years.

GUS: Yes, we can add up, you know.

LYNNIE: How did you find me?

ROLAND: I went through records, birth certificates, traced you.

GUS: And here she is.

ROLAND: I've brought her back to you. Lynette this is your mother. Talk to her.

LYNNIE: I don't want to talk to her.

> BONNY *gets up and goes to the door, looks into another room.*

GUS: You lost something?

LYNNIE: What are you looking for?

GUS: I know what she's looking for.

ROLAND: Sit down. Are you cold?

BONNY: Yes.

ROLAND: It's very cold here.

LYNNIE: Look. It's really nice, what you've done. But I don't think it will work out.

ROLAND: She's your mother.

LYNNIE: I know that.

ROLAND: I've brought her back.

LYNNIE: Like I said, it's very nice of you but—

> BONNY *has gone to the door again.*

GUS: There she goes again.

ROLAND: Bonny, what is it?

LYNNIE: It's the kid she wants back, the boy. He didn't want a kid, he wasn't ready. It was the wrong time. We had to start properly. He found a job. We came out here.

GUS: A job? Mixing chemicals. Look what it did to me. Look at my skin, my hands. The skin falls off, tears off, hangs in sheets, my arms bleed all the time. I breathed it in, it's in my lungs. Some job.

LYNNIE: Take her away.

GUS: Only took the job to get away from her. Didn't think for a minute she'd give the kid away. But bang, she did and we've been getting over it ever since.

LYNNIE: Please.

GUS: Except we don't.

LYNNIE: Go.

GUS: Get over it.

LYNNIE: She doesn't want me. I don't want her.

BONNY 's at the door again.

GUS: She's like a dog at a bone, isn't she?

ROLAND: Talk to her.

GUS: Yeah, talk to her.

LYNNIE: He's not here. I gave him away. To have a life. A life away from you. My own life, I could do what I wanted, free. All you did was spy on me, watch every move, keep me prisoner. She drove me crazy, made me leave. I gave up the kid to get away from her and now you want me to say, 'Hello, I love you anyway'?

She brings out a tin of photos.

You want me to make the past sixteen years disappear? No. Here.

She tosses the photos into the air. ROLAND *and* BONNY *search through them frantically.*

I brought this stuff with me. Hanging on to something. But I don't want this either. This isn't my life. Not my life.

ROLAND: [*showing a photo to her*] The man in this photograph. Who is it?

LYNNIE: What's it to you?

ROLAND: Do you know who this is?

LYNNIE: It's my father, alright?

ROLAND: Lynnie, listen to me. This is my father too.

LYNNIE: How can that be your father?

ROLAND: It is.

LYNNIE: I know who my father was.

ROLAND: So do I. We had the same father. You're my sister.

LYNNIE: Is that why you're here?

GUS: I think it's time you went.

ROLAND: I'm your brother.

LYNNIE: Is that why you dragged her here?

GUS: Leave, you hear me?

ROLAND: Your brother.

LYNNIE: Stop doing this to me! I don't care who you are. I don't

want a brother. I don't want her. Understand? You want to
make me go all the way back to the beginning again. No! I
want my life to start!

GUS: Come on talk to her. [*He drags* LYNNIE *to* BONNY] So you
want your daughter back do you?

BONNY: Yes.

GUS: You hated her didn't you?

BONNY: Yes.

GUS: It was the kid you wanted to see wasn't it?

BONNY: Yes.

GUS: You're an old cunt aren't you?

BONNY: Yes.

GUS: You want to kiss and make up now? You want us all to be
one big happy family?

BONNY: [*screaming*] YES!

ROLAND: [*screaming*] STOP!

LYNNIE: I want my life to start!

> *Thunder clap, darkness, howling wind.*

SCENE SIXTEEN

Open country, howling wind.

ROLAND: Go back to the car. I said go back to the car. I want to
stay out here. By myself. Let go. Let go of me. I saw my sister.
She was standing there. I looked right into her eyes and she
turned away. We were together. Why won't you let go of me?

BONNY: Yes.

ROLAND: Go back, leave me here … Let go … Don't you
understand?

BONNY: Yes.

ROLAND: Why won't you leave me alone?

BONNY: Yes.

> *She grabs* ROLAND*'s head with her hands and stares into
> his eyes. The wind suddenly peaks and dies.* ROLAND *cries
> out. Silence.*

ROLAND: I can't help you, can I?

BONNY: Yes.

ROLAND: I can't save you, can I?

BONNY: Yes.

ROLAND: Listen. Listen. I'm sorry. You have to go back, don't you?

BONNY: Yes.

ROLAND: I have to take you back, don't I?

BONNY: Yes.

ROLAND: Back there, that place?

BONNY: Yes.

ROLAND: With nothing?

BONNY: Yes.

SCENE SEVENTEEN

Roland's place.

CHRIS: I called around twice before. No-one home. I just sat in the milkbar and stared at the ocean. Thought if I just sat there you'd walk past. I miss you, Roland, where have you been?

ROLAND: Inland.

CHRIS: You miss me?

ROLAND: Yes.

CHRIS: I hated the way I just couldn't see you. I worried about you. I worried that you'd worry. About me. But I didn't do anything desperate. Thought about it. This guy I have to see, he sees these other kids. They've tried. Not me. First few times, I was waiting for them to strap on the wires and turn up the voltage. Make me stare at ink blots for hours. But nothing like that. Just questions. You been to a shrink?

ROLAND: Yes.

CHRIS: Boring more than anything. But I put up with it. Kept quiet. You finished what you were writing.

ROLAND: Yes.

CHRIS: That's good Roland. Only one person knows I'm here, this girl who goes to the same place. But I trust her. She's great. Getting here was very interesting. Had to cover my tracks. Cover up the cover-up. Make up stories to back up the stories I told them. It's worked up till now. But I won't risk it again. I can't see you. Not for a while. Like a few years. But I learnt how to do it, cover up. Lie low. Like I'm a counter agent sent over to the enemy pretending I'm on their side. Then one day I'll get the call and start my work. And they have no idea how dangerous I really am. They were unbelievable in the sessions we had together. Mum was like this crazy woman. Same nice clothes, same jewellery, same hair do. But crazy. Dad just silent. Nothing. And when we got right down to it, the thing they hated most was that they've been robbed of grandchildren.

ROLAND: Have they?

CHRIS: Fucked if I know Roland, fucked if I know anything. And it's great. Who knows what I might do?

ROLAND: I'm in the presence of someone who's passed through the fires of hell.

CHRIS: No. No, not that bad. If I don't go I'll be late. All my careful stories'll fall apart. You look after yourself. Off I go, into hiding.

SCENE EIGHTEEN

Theatre foyer. A bell rings. ROLAND *paces, lights a cigarette. The* FRIENDS *from Scene Three enter.*

FRIEND ONE: Here he is.

FRIEND TWO: Roland?

ROLAND: Hello.

FRIEND THREE: You watching tonight?

ROLAND: No. I'll walk around, come back for the end.

FRIEND ONE: You'll be fine. Won't he?

FRIEND THREE: Of course he will.

> CONNIE *enters with an enormous bunch of flowers. She hands it to* ROLAND.

CONNIE: All the best.

ROLAND: Thank you very much.

Another bell rings.

FRIEND ONE: Come on gang.

They go. CONNIE *lingers a moment, then exits.* ROLAND *leaves by the opposite door, listening to the distorted sounds of an expectant audience.*

SCENE NINETEEN

Old people's home. ROLAND *enters smoking a cigarette. He looks around the room, then sits. After a moment* BONNY *comes in.*

BONNY: [*exactly as* KATHLEEN *in Scene One*] And where have you been?

THE END

www.ingramcontent.com/pod-product-compliance
Lightning Source LLC
Chambersburg PA
CBHW050028090426
42734CB00021B/3469